I0815258

DRINKS!

Publications International, Ltd.

Louis Weber, CEO
Publications International, Ltd.
8140 Lehigh Ave
Morton Grove, IL 60053

Pictured on the front cover *(clockwise from top left):* Apple-K Juice *(page 35)*, Sangria *(page 86)*, Espresso Shake *(page 167)*, Strawberry Sundae Shake *(page 173)*, Chocolate Cake Shake *(page 152)* and Grasshopper *(page 108)*.

Pictured on the back cover *(clockwise from top left):* Blueberry Pineapple Smoothie *(page 7)*, Frozen Mudslide *(page 122)*, Blue Hawaii *(page 106)*, Strawberry-Basil Sparklers *(page 128)*, Cucumber Basil Cooler *(page 53)*, Key Lime Chiller *(page 161)* and White Sangria *(page 81)*.

ISBN: 978-1-63938-835-6

Manufactured in China.

8 7 6 5 4 3 2 1

WARNING: Food preparation, baking and cooking involve inherent dangers: misuse of electric products, sharp electric tools, boiling water, hot stoves, allergic reactions, foodborne illnesses and the like, pose numerous potential risks. Publications International, Ltd. (PIL) assumes no responsibility or liability for any damages you may experience as a result of following recipes, instructions, tips or advice in this publication.

While we hope this publication helps you find new ways to eat delicious foods, you may not always achieve the results desired due to variations in ingredients, cooking temperatures, typos, errors, omissions or individual cooking abilities.

According to the Surgeon General, women should not drink alcoholic beverages during pregnancy because of the risk of birth defects. Consumption of alcoholic beverages impairs your ability to drive a car or operate machinery and may cause health problems. If you drink, do not drive.

Let's get social!

 @Publications_International

 @PublicationsInternational

www.pilbooks.com

CONTENTS

SMOOTHIES

Wow Watermelon Smoothie

makes 2 servings

- 2 tablespoons sugar
- 4½ cups cubed seedless watermelon
- 1½ cups strawberry sorbet
- 1 banana
- 1½ cups ice cubes

1. Place sugar in small shallow dish. Moisten rims of two glasses; dip rims in sugar.
2. Combine watermelon, sorbet, banana and ice in blender; process until smooth.
3. Pour into prepared glasses; serve immediately.

Island Delight Smoothie

makes 4 servings

- 2 cups chopped fresh or jarred mango
- 1 container (16 ounces) plain yogurt
- 1½ cups cold pineapple-orange juice
- 1 cup chopped pineapple
- 1 frozen banana
- ½ cup sliced fresh strawberries
- 2 tablespoons honey
- 1½ cups ice cubes
- Fresh banana slices

1. Combine mango, yogurt, pineapple-orange juice, pineapple, frozen banana, strawberries, honey and ice in blender; blend until smooth.
2. Pour into four glasses. Garnish with banana slices; serve immediately.

Blueberry Pineapple Smoothie

makes 2 servings

2 cups fresh or frozen blueberries, plus additional for garnish
1½ cups diced pineapple
1 cup pineapple juice
1 to 3 ice cubes
Pineapple chunks

1 Combine 2 cups blueberries, diced pineapple and pineapple juice in blender; blend until smooth. Add 3 ice cubes if using fresh fruit or 1 to 2 ice cubes if using frozen fruit; blend until smooth.

2 Pour into two glasses. Garnish with additional blueberries and pineapple chunks; serve immediately.

Banana Split Smoothie

makes 4 servings

- 1 banana
- ¼ cup milk
- 5 maraschino cherries, plus additional for garnish
- 1 tablespoon chocolate syrup
- ⅛ teaspoon coconut extract
- 4 cups chocolate frozen yogurt

1 Combine banana, milk, 5 cherries, chocolate syrup and coconut extract in blender; blend until smooth. Add yogurt, 1 cup at a time; process after each addition until smooth and thick.

2 Pour into four glasses. Garnish with additional maraschino cherries; serve immediately.

Berry-Banana Breakfast Smoothie

makes 2 servings

- 1 container (6 ounces) berry-flavored yogurt
- 1 banana
- ½ cup milk
- 4 ice cubes

1. Combine yogurt, banana, milk and ice in blender; blend until smooth.
2. Pour into two glasses; serve immediately.

S'more Dessert Smoothie

makes 2 servings

1 cup vanilla frozen yogurt
1 cup chocolate frozen yogurt
½ cup milk
2 to 3 ice cubes
¼ cup mini marshmallows
¼ cup mini semisweet chocolate chips
1 graham cracker, divided
Whipped cream

1 Combine frozen yogurt, milk and ice in blender; blend until smooth. Add marshmallows and chocolate chips; blend until just combined. Pulse in ½ graham cracker.

2 Pour into two glasses. Crush remaining graham cracker half. Top with whipped cream and crushed cracker crumbs; serve immediately.

Blueberry Banana Oatmeal Smoothie

makes 2 servings

1 cup milk
1 banana
½ cup frozen blueberries
½ cup plain yogurt
¼ cup quick oats

1. Combine milk, banana and blueberries in blender; blend until smooth. Add yogurt and oats; blend until smooth.
2. Pour into two glasses; serve immediately.

Vermont Maple Smoothie

makes 4 servings

- 1½ cups unsweetened applesauce
- 1 cup vanilla frozen yogurt
- 1 cup milk
- 3 tablespoons maple syrup
- ½ teaspoon ground cinnamon
- 2 ice cubes
- Ground nutmeg

1. Combine applesauce, frozen yogurt, milk, maple syrup, cinnamon and ice in blender; blend until smooth.
2. Pour into four glasses. Sprinkle with nutmeg; serve immediately.

Raspberry Cocoa Freeze

makes 2 servings

½ cup frozen raspberries
½ cup vanilla frozen yogurt
⅓ cup milk
1 teaspoon unsweetened cocoa powder
Fresh raspberries

1. Place frozen raspberries, frozen yogurt, milk and cocoa powder in blender; blend until smooth.
2. Pour into two glasses. Garnish with fresh raspberries; serve immediately.

Spiced Maple Banana Oatmeal Smoothie

makes 2 servings

1 frozen banana
½ cup ice cubes
½ cup plain yogurt
¼ cup quick oats
¼ cup milk
1 tablespoon maple syrup, plus additional for garnish
Dash ground cinnamon
Dash ground nutmeg
Whipped cream and cinnamon stick

1. Combine banana, ice, yogurt, oats, milk, 1 tablespoon maple syrup, cinnamon and nutmeg in blender; blend until smooth.
2. Pour into two glasses. Garnish with whipped cream and cinnamon stick. Drizzle with additional maple syrup; serve immediately.

Raspberry Peach Smoothie

makes 2 servings

- 1½ cups fresh or frozen peach slices, plus additional for garnish
- 1 cup peach nectar
- 1 container (6 ounces) raspberry yogurt
- ¾ cup fresh or frozen raspberries, plus additional for garnish
- 1 tablespoon honey
- 1 to 3 ice cubes

1. Combine peaches, nectar, yogurt, raspberries and honey in blender; blend until smooth. Add 3 ice cubes if using fresh fruit and 1 to 2 ice cubes if using frozen fruit; blend until smooth.
2. Pour into two glasses. Garnish with additional peaches and raspberries; serve immediately.

Pineapple Crush

makes 2 servings

- 1½ cups frozen pineapple chunks
- ½ cup coconut milk
- ½ cup milk
- ½ cup plain yogurt
- 2 ice cubes
- 2 teaspoons sugar
- 1 teaspoon vanilla
- Pineapple wedges

1. Combine pineapple, coconut milk, milk, yogurt, ice, sugar and vanilla in blender; blend until smooth.
2. Pour mixture into two glasses. Garnish with pineapple wedges; serve immediately.

"Hot" Chocolate Smoothie

makes 4 servings

- 2½ cups chocolate frozen yogurt
- 1¾ cups chocolate soy milk
- 1 banana
- ⅛ teaspoon chipotle chili powder
- 1½ cups ice cubes
- Whipped cream and chocolate shavings

1. Combine frozen yogurt, soy milk, banana, chili powder and ice in blender; blend until smooth.
2. Pour into four glasses. Garnish with whipped cream and chocolate shavings; serve immediately.

Mango-Ginger Smoothie

makes 4 servings

- 2 cups cubed fresh or jarred mango
- 2½ cups fresh peeled sliced peaches *or* 1 package (16 ounces) frozen sliced peaches
- 1 container (6 ounces) vanilla yogurt
- 2 tablespoons honey
- 2 teaspoons fresh grated ginger
- 1 cup ice cubes

1. Combine mango, peaches, yogurt, honey, ginger and ice in blender; blend until smooth.
2. Pour into four glasses; serve immediately.

Cranberry Orange Smoothie

makes 2 servings

- **2 cups fresh or frozen peach slices**
- **1¼ cups orange juice**
- **½ cup whole berry cranberry sauce**
- **1 to 3 ice cubes**
- **Fresh orange slices and cranberries**

1 Combine peaches, orange juice and cranberry sauce in blender; blend until smooth. Add 3 ice cubes if using fresh fruit or 1 to 2 ice cubes if using frozen fruit; blend until smooth.

2 Pour into two glasses. Garnish with orange slices and cranberries; serve immediately.

Honey-Nut Smoothie

makes 2 servings

- 1 cup vanilla frozen yogurt
- 1 banana
- ½ cup milk
- ½ cup creamy peanut butter
- 1 tablespoon honey
- 1 cup ice cubes

1. Combine yogurt, bananas, milk, peanut butter, honey and ice in blender; blend until smooth.
2. Pour into two glasses; serve immediately.

Coconut Smoothie

makes 1 serving

- 1 cup coconut sorbet
- ½ cup coconut milk
- ¼ cup crushed ice
- 3 tablespoons sweetened flaked coconut, divided
- 1 tablespoon honey, divided

1. Combine sorbet, coconut milk, ice, 2 tablespoons coconut flakes and ½ tablespoon honey in blender; blend until smooth.
2. Dip rim of glass into remaining ½ tablespoon honey, and then dip into remaining 1 tablespoon coconut. Pour smoothie into prepared glass; serve immediately.

Dreamsicle Smoothie

makes 4 servings

- 1½ cups vanilla yogurt
- ¾ cup frozen orange juice concentrate
- ½ cup milk
- ¼ teaspoon vanilla
- 2 cups ice cubes
- Whipped cream and orange slices

1. Combine yogurt, juice concentrate, milk, vanilla and ice in blender; blend until smooth.
2. Pour into four glasses. Garnish with whipped cream and orange slices; serve immediately.

Grapefruit Smoothie

makes 2 servings

- 3 tablespoons sugar, divided
- 1 to 2 drops red food coloring (optional)
- 1 red grapefruit, peeled and seeded with membrane removed
- 1 cup ice cubes
- ¼ to ½ cup grapefruit juice
- Sprigs fresh lavender or rosemary

1. Combine 1 tablespoon sugar and food coloring in small bowl, if desired; stir until evenly tinted. Moisten rims of two glasses; dip in red sugar.
2. Combine grapefruit, ice, grapefruit juice and remaining 2 tablespoons sugar in blender or food processor; blend until smooth.
3. Pour into prepared glasses. Garnish with lavender sprigs; serve immediately.

Cinnamon-Apple Smoothie

makes 4 servings

- 2 Gala, Braeburn or other apples, peeled, cored and thinly sliced
- 2 cups ice cubes
- 2 bananas
- 1 container (6 ounces) vanilla yogurt
- ¾ cup apple juice
- 2 teaspoons ground cinnamon, plus additional for garnish
- Whipped cream and apple slices

1 Combine apples, ice, bananas, yogurt, apple juice and 2 teaspoons cinnamon in blender; blend until smooth.

2 Pour into four glasses. Garnish with whipped cream, apple slices and additional cinnamon; serve immediately.

Peachy Razz Refresher

makes 2 servings

- 1 cup ice cubes
- 1 cup frozen sliced peaches
- ½ cup frozen raspberries
- ½ cup plain yogurt
- ½ cup orange juice
- Fresh peach slices and/or fresh raspberries

1 Combine ice, peaches, frozen raspberries, yogurt and orange juice in blender; blend until smooth.

2 Pour into two glasses. Garnish with peach slices and fresh raspberries; serve immediately.

Peachy Mango Smoothie

makes 2 servings

1 cup frozen sliced peaches
1 cup frozen mango chunks
½ cup orange juice
½ cup plain yogurt
Fresh peach slices

1 Combine frozen peaches, mango, ½ cup orange juice and yogurt in blender; blend until smooth.

2 Pour into two glasses. Garnish with fresh peach slices; serve immediately.

Spiced Passion Fruit Smoothie

makes 3 servings

- 1 cup vanilla Greek yogurt
- 1 cup sliced fresh strawberries
- 1 banana
- ¼ cup frozen passion fruit juice concentrate, thawed
- ¾ teaspoon pumpkin pie spice
- ⅛ teaspoon ground white pepper

1. Combine yogurt, strawberries, banana, juice concentrate, pumpkin pie spice and white pepper in blender; blend until smooth.
2. Pour into three glasses; serve immediately.

Cantaloupe Smoothie

makes 4 servings

- **3 cups cubed cantaloupe**
- **2 containers (6 ounces each) orange yogurt**
- **½ cup cold orange-tangerine juice or orange juice**
- **1 tablespoon honey**
- **1 teaspoon vanilla**
- **4 small cantaloupe wedges and orange peel twists**

1. Combine cubed cantaloupe, yogurt, juice, honey and vanilla in blender; blend until smooth.
2. Pour into four glasses. Garnish with cantaloupe wedges and orange peel; serve immediately.

Honeydew Ginger Smoothie

makes 2 servings

- 1½ cups cubed honeydew melon
- 1 banana
- ½ cup vanilla yogurt
- ½ cup ice cubes
- ¼ teaspoon grated fresh ginger
- Honeydew melon balls and fresh ginger slices

1. Combine honeydew, banana, yogurt, ice and grated ginger in blender; blend until smooth.
2. Pour into two glasses. Garnish with melon balls and ginger slices; serve immediately.

Peanut Butter Banana Blend

makes 2 servings

1 frozen banana
½ cup plain yogurt
½ cup milk
1 tablespoon peanut butter
Banana slices

1. Combine banana, yogurt, milk and peanut butter in blender; blend until smooth.
2. Pour into two glasses. Garnish with banana slices; serve immediately.

Black Forest Smoothie

makes 1 serving

1 container (6 ounces) cherry yogurt
½ cup frozen dark sweet cherries
¼ cup milk
2 tablespoons sugar
2 tablespoons unsweetened cocoa powder
¼ teaspoon almond extract
1 to 2 ice cubes

1. Combine yogurt, cherries, milk, sugar, cocoa, almond extract and ice in blender; blend until smooth.
2. Pour into glass; serve immediately.

JUICES

Apple-K Juice

makes 2 servings

1 kiwi, peeled
1 apple
4 leaves kale
1 stalk celery
½ lemon, peeled

Juice kiwi, apple, kale, celery and lemon. Stir.

Sweet Green Pineapple Juice

makes 1 serving

¼ pineapple, peeled
1 cup broccoli florets
1 carrot

Juice pineapple, broccoli and carrot. Stir.

Red Orange Juice

makes 2 servings

- 1 orange, peeled
- 1 apple
- ½ cup raspberries
- ½ cup strawberries

Juice orange, apple, raspberries and strawberries. Stir.

Tropical Twist Juice

makes 2 servings

⅛ pineapple, peeled
⅛ seedless watermelon, rind removed
1 orange, peeled
½ mango, peeled
⅓ cup strawberries

Juice pineapple, watermelon, orange, mango and strawberries. Stir.

Workout Warmup Juice

makes 2 servings

2 apples
2 kiwis, peeled
4 leaves kale
½ lime, peeled

Juice apples, kiwis, kale and lime. Stir.

Spicy Apple Peach Juice

makes 3 servings

2 apples
6 leaves mustard greens
2 stalks celery
1 kiwi, peeled
1 peach

Juice apples, mustard greens, celery, kiwi and peach. Stir.

Orchard Crush Juice

makes 2 servings

2 apples
1 cup fresh raspberries
1 cup fresh strawberries

Juice apples, raspberries and strawberries. Stir.

Melon Refresher

makes 2 servings

- ¼ cantaloupe, rind removed
- 1 pear
- 1 lime, peeled
- 2 sprigs fresh mint

Juice cantaloupe, pear, lime and mint. Stir.

Sweet Green Grape Juice

makes 2 servings

- ¼ honeydew melon, rind removed
- 2 kiwi, peeled
- ½ cup green seedless grapes

Juice honeydew, kiwi and grapes. Stir.

Sharp Apple Cooler

makes 3 servings

3 apples
1 cucumber
¼ cup fresh mint
1 inch fresh ginger, peeled

Juice apples, cucumber, mint and ginger. Stir.

Melonade

makes 4 servings

¼ seedless watermelon, rind removed
1 apple
1 lemon, peeled

Juice watermelon, apple and lemon. Stir.

Cool Apple Mango Juice

makes 2 servings

1 mango, peeled
1 apple
1 cucumber
½ inch fresh ginger, peeled

Juice mango, apple, cucumber and ginger. Stir.

Triple Green Juice

makes 2 servings

- ½ honeydew melon, rind removed
- 1 cucumber
- 4 leaves kale

Juice honeydew, cucumber and kale. Stir.

Orchard Medley Juice

makes 3 servings

- ½ cup water
- 2 plums, pitted and cut into chunks
- 1 sweet red apple, seeded and cut into chunks
- 1 pear, seeded and cut into chunks
- 2 teaspoons lemon juice

Combine water, plums, apple, pear and lemon juice in blender; blend until smooth. Serve immediately.

Double Green Pineapple Juice

makes 1 serving

4 leaves Swiss chard
4 leaves kale
¼ pineapple, peeled

Juice chard, kale and pineapple. Stir.

Cool Cucumber Juice

makes 2 servings

- 1 cucumber
- ¼ pineapple, peeled
- ¼ cup fresh cilantro

Juice cucumber, pineapple and cilantro. Stir.

Tangerapple Juice

makes 2 servings

2 apples
2 tangerines, peeled
¼ lemon, peeled

Juice apples, tangerines and lemon. Stir.

Citrus Carrot Juice

makes 2 servings

1 orange, peeled
2 carrots
½ lemon, peeled

Juice orange, carrots and lemon. Stir.

Cucumber Basil Cooler

makes 2 servings

- 1 cucumber
- 1 apple
- ½ cup fresh basil
- ½ lime, peeled

Juice cucumber, apple, basil and lime. Stir.

Wheatgrass Blast

makes 2 servings

- 2 apples
- 2 cups wheatgrass
- 1 lemon, peeled
- 6 sprigs fresh mint

Juice apples, wheatgrass, lemon and mint. Stir.

Island Orange Juice

makes 2 servings

2 oranges, peeled
2 guavas
½ cup strawberries

Juice oranges, guavas and strawberries. Stir.

Sweet and Spicy Citrus Juice

makes 2 servings

- 5 carrots
- 1 orange *or* 2 clementines, peeled
- ⅓ cup strawberries
- 1 lemon, peeled
- ½ inch fresh ginger, peeled

Juice carrots, orange, strawberries, lemon and ginger. Stir.

Cleansing Green Juice

makes 2 servings

- 4 leaves bok choy
- 1 stalk celery
- ½ cucumber
- ¼ bulb fennel
- ½ lemon, peeled

Juice bok choy, celery, cucumber, fennel and lemon. Stir.

TEA & COFFEE

Mocha Java Spice Lattes

makes 4 servings

- **⅓ cup whipping cream**
- **⅓ cup semisweet chocolate chips**
- **3 cups freshly brewed strong coffee**
- **1 tablespoon sugar**
- **⅛ teaspoon pumpkin pie spice, plus additional for garnish**
- **Whipped cream**

1 Bring cream to a simmer in medium saucepan over medium heat. Add chips; stir until well blended. Add coffee, sugar and ⅛ teaspoon pumpkin pie spice. Whisk until blended; bring to a simmer.

2 Divide mixture among four coffee mugs. Top with whipped cream and sprinkle with additional pumpkin pie spice.

Almond Milk Tea with Tapioca

makes 2 servings

- 3½ cups water
- 2 black tea bags
- 4 teaspoons sugar
- ¼ teaspoon almond extract
- 1 tablespoon quick-cooking tapioca
- 4 tablespoons whole milk
- Ice cubes

1 Bring water to a boil in medium saucepan over medium-high heat.

2 Pour 2 cups boiling water over tea bags in teapot or 2-cup heatproof measuring cup. Steep tea 4 minutes. Remove and discard tea bags. Stir in sugar and almond extract; cool to room temperature.

3 Meanwhile, returning remaining 1½ cups water to a boil over medium-high heat; stir in tapioca. Boil 3 to 4 minutes or until tapioca is translucent and cooked through. Drain tapioca in fine-mesh strainer; rinse under cold water until cool.

4 Divide tapioca between two tall glasses; pour 2 tablespoons milk into each glass. Fill each glass three-fourths full with ice. Divide tea between glasses; stir to combine. Serve immediately.

Viennese Coffee

makes 4 servings

- **1 cup whipping cream, divided**
- **1 teaspoon powdered sugar**
- **3 ounces bittersweet or semisweet chocolate, chopped *or* ½ cup chocolate chips**
- **3 cups strong freshly brewed hot coffee**
- **¼ cup crème de cacao or Irish cream liqueur (optional)**
- **Shaved chocolate**

1 Combine ⅔ cup cream and powdered sugar in large bowl of electric mixer. Beat at high speed until soft peaks form. Cover and refrigerate until ready to use (up to 8 hours). If mixture has separated slightly, whisk lightly with wire whisk before using.

2 Bring remaining ⅓ cup cream to a boil in small heavy saucepan over medium-low heat. Add chocolate; remove from heat. Let stand 5 minutes or until chocolate is melted; stir until smooth.

3 Add hot coffee to chocolate mixture. Heat over low heat just until bubbles form around edge of pan and coffee is heated through, stirring frequently. Remove from heat; stir in crème de cacao, if desired.

4 Pour into four mugs. Top with whipped cream and garnish with chocolate shavings.

Green Tea Lychee Frappé

makes 2 servings

1 can (15 ounces) lychees in syrup,* undrained
2 cups water
2 slices peeled fresh ginger (2×¼ inches)
3 green tea bags
Fresh orange slices and cherries

Canned lychees are readily available in either the canned fruit or ethnic foods section of most large supermarkets.

1 Drain lychees, reserving syrup. Place lychees in single layer in medium resealable food storage bag; freeze 1 hour or until firm. Cover syrup; refrigerate.

2 Bring water and ginger to a boil in small saucepan over medium-high heat. Pour over tea bags in teapot or 2-cup heatproof measuring cup; steep 3 minutes. Discard ginger and tea bags. Cool to room temperature; refrigerate until cool.

3 Combine frozen lychees, chilled green tea and ½ cup reserved syrup in blender or food processor; blend 20 seconds or until smooth.

4 Pour into two glasses. Garnish with orange slices and cherries. Serve immediately.

Hot Chocolate Coffee

makes 4 to 6 servings

6 cups water
½ cup ground dark roast coffee
1 cup half-and-half
⅓ cup chocolate syrup
¼ cup packed dark brown sugar
1½ teaspoons vanilla, divided
1 cup whipping cream
¼ cup powdered sugar
Ground cinnamon

1 Place water in drip coffee maker. Place coffee in filter basket of coffee maker. Combine half-and-half, chocolate syrup, brown sugar and 1 teaspoon vanilla in coffee pot. Place coffee pot with cream mixture in coffee maker. Brew coffee; coffee will drip into chocolate mixture.

2 Meanwhile, beat cream in medium bowl with electric mixer at high speed until soft peaks form. Add powdered sugar and remaining ½ teaspoon vanilla; beat until stiff peaks form. Pour coffee into mugs; top with whipped cream. Sprinkle with ground cinnamon.

Peach Iced Tea

makes 4 servings

- 4 cups water
- 3 black tea bags
- ¼ cup sugar
- 1 can (about 11 ounces) peach nectar
- 1 cup frozen peach slices
- Ice cubes

1. Bring water to a boil in medium saucepan over high heat. Remove from heat; add tea bags and let steep 5 minutes. Remove tea bags; stir in sugar until dissolved. Cool to room temperature.
2. Stir in peach nectar and peach slices. Refrigerate until cold. Serve over ice.

Sparkling Tangerine-Cranberry Green Tea

makes 4 servings

- 2 cups water
- 2 green tea bags
- 1 cup tangerine juice (3 to 4 tangerines)
- ½ cup cold cranberry juice
- 1 cup cold seltzer water
- Ice cubes
- Tangerine slices and/or fresh cranberries

1. Bring water to a boil in medium saucepan over high heat. Remove from heat; add tea bags and let steep 5 minutes. Remove tea bags; cool completely. Pour tea into large pitcher; stir in juices and seltzer.
2. Serve over ice; garnish with tangerine slices and/or cranberries.

Iced Mexican Coffee

makes 6 servings

½ cup ground dark roast coffee
4 cups water
1 tablespoon sugar
⅔ cup half-and-half or milk
¼ cup chocolate syrup
1 teaspoon vanilla
½ teaspoon cinnamon extract or ground cinnamon*
Ice cubes

Or omit cinnamon extract and break two 3-inch-long cinnamon sticks into several pieces. Place cinnamon pieces in filter basket of coffee maker with ground coffee.

1 Place ground coffee in filter basket of coffee maker. Add water to coffee maker; brew coffee. Pour coffee into 4-cup heatproof measuring cup or small pitcher. Add sugar; stir until dissolved. Cover; cool to room temperature.

2 Combine half-and-half, chocolate syrup, vanilla and cinnamon extract in pitcher; mix well. Stir in cooled coffee. Serve over ice.

Melon Bubble Tea

makes 5 servings

- **6 cups water**
- **2 green tea bags**
- **⅓ cup sugar**
- **½ cup black or pastel tapioca pearls***
- **4 cups cubed melon (cantaloupe, honeydew or watermelon)**
- **2 cups orange juice**
- **½ cup canned coconut milk**
- **4 cups ice cubes**

Large specialty tapioca pearls specifically designed for bubble teas are available in Asian markets and gourmet food stores.

1. Bring water to a boil in medium saucepan over high heat. Place tea bags in 2-cup heatproof measuring cup; pour 2 cups water over tea bags. Steep 5 minutes. Remove tea bags; stir in sugar until dissolved. Cool completely; refrigerate until ready to use.
2. Meanwhile, return remaining 4 cups water to a boil over high heat; gently stir in tapioca pearls, allowing pearls to float to top. Reduce heat to low; simmer, uncovered, 25 minutes.
3. Remove from heat; let stand 25 minutes or until pearls are chewy and translucent. Drain and rinse under cold water. Pour tea into large pitcher; stir in pearls.
4. Working in batches, combine melon, orange juice, coconut milk and ice in blender or food processor; blend until smooth.
5. Place ¼ cup tapioca mixture in bottom of five glasses. Top evenly with melon mixture; serve immediately.

Iced Cappuccino

makes 2 servings

1 cup vanilla frozen yogurt or vanilla ice cream

1 cup cold strong brewed coffee or cold brew

2 teaspoons sugar

1 teaspoon unsweetened cocoa powder

1 teaspoon vanilla

1. Combine all ingredients in blender or food processor; blend until smooth. Place container in freezer; freeze 1½ to 2 hours or until top and sides of mixture are partially frozen.
2. Scrape sides of container; blend until smooth and frothy.
3. Pour into two glasses; serve immediately.

Iced Mocha Cappuccino: Increase amount of cocoa to 1 tablespoon. Proceed as directed above.

Tip: To add an extra flavor boost to this refreshing drink, add orange peel, lemon peel or a dash of ground cinnamon to your coffee grounds before brewing.

Spiced Raspberry Tea Mix

makes 4 cups mix (64 servings)

- 2 cups sugar
- 1½ cups instant unsweetened tea
- 8 packets (0.23 ounces each) raspberry-flavored unsweetened drink mix
- ¼ cup lemonade drink mix
- 2 teaspoons ground cardamom
- 2 teaspoons ground cinnamon
- 2 teaspoons ground ginger
- 1 teaspoon ground allspice
- 1½ cups water
- Fresh raspberries and orange slices

1. Combine sugar, tea, drink mixes, cardamom, cinnamon, ginger and allspice in large bowl; whisk to combine.
2. Bring water to a boil in small saucepan. Stir in 2 tablespoons of tea mixture until dissolved. Store remaining tea mixture in airtight container.
3. Pour tea into two ice-filled glasses. Garnish with raspberries and orange slices.

Pumpkin Spice Latte

makes 2 servings

1¾ cups milk, divided
½ cup canned pumpkin
3 tablespoons packed brown sugar
1 teaspoon grated fresh ginger
1 teaspoon pumpkin pie spice
½ teaspoon ground cinnamon, plus additional for garnish
¼ teaspoon salt
⅛ teaspoon coarsely ground black pepper
1 cup strong-brewed hot coffee*
1 tablespoon vanilla
Whipped cream

Use about 1 tablespoon ground espresso roast or other dark roast coffee for each 3 ounces of water.

1 Combine ½ cup milk, pumpkin, brown sugar, ginger, pumpkin pie spice, ½ teaspoon cinnamon, salt and pepper in medium saucepan; whisk until well blended. Cook over medium-low heat 10 minutes, whisking frequently. Remove from heat; whisk in coffee and vanilla. Strain through fine-mesh strainer into medium bowl.

2 Bring remaining 1¼ cups milk to a simmer in small saucepan over medium-high heat. For froth, whisk vigorously 30 seconds. Whisk into coffee mixture until blended. Garnish with whipped cream and additional cinnamon.

PUNCHES & PITCHERS

White Sangria

makes 8 to 10 servings

- 2 oranges, cut into ¼-inch slices
- 2 lemons, cut into ¼-inch slices
- ½ cup sugar
- 2 bottles (750 ml each) cold dry white wine
- ½ cup peach schnapps
- 3 ripe peaches, pitted and cut into wedges
- Ice cubes

1. Place orange and lemon slices in large pitcher or punch bowl. Pour sugar over fruit; mash lightly until sugar dissolves and fruit begins to break down.
2. Stir in wine, schnapps and peaches; mix well. Refrigerate at least 2 hours or overnight. Serve over ice.

Piña Colada Punch

makes 8 to 10 servings

- 3 cups water
- 10 whole cloves
- 4 cardamom pods
- 2 cinnamon sticks
- 1 pint piña colada frozen yogurt, softened*
- 1 can (12 ounces) frozen pineapple juice concentrate, thawed
- 1¼ cups cold lemon seltzer water or lemon-line soda
- 1¼ teaspoons rum extract
- ¾ teaspoon coconut extract (optional)

***Or substitute pineapple sherbet and use the coconut extract.**

1 Combine water, cloves, cardamom and cinnamon in small saucepan; bring to a boil over high heat. Reduce heat to low; cover and simmer 5 minutes. Cool to room temperature; strain out and discard spices.

2 Combine spiced water, frozen yogurt and juice concentrate in small punch bowl or pitcher; stir until frozen yogurt is melted. Stir in seltzer water, rum extract and coconut extract, if desired.

Cranberry-Orange Party Punch

makes 16 servings

Orange Cranberry Ice Ring

- 1 medium seedless orange, cut into wedges
- ½ to ¾ cup fresh or thawed frozen cranberries
- 3 cups apple cider

Punch

- 2 quarts cranberry juice cocktail
- 4 cups apple cider
- 1 can (12 ounces) frozen orange juice concentrate, thawed
- 1 can (12 ounces) frozen apple juice or apple-berry juice concentrate
- ¼ teaspoon red food coloring (optional)
- 1 bottle (2 liters) cold lemon-lime soda or ginger ale

1 The day before serving, arrange orange wedges and cranberries in 3½-cup ring mold; fill with 3 cups cider. Freeze until solid, about 8 hours or overnight.

2 When ready to serve, combine cranberry juice, 4 cups apple cider, orange juice concentrate, apple juice concentrate and food coloring, if desired, in large punch bowl; stir to blend well. Pour in soda.

3 To unmold ice ring, dip bottom of mold briefly in hot water; float in punch.

Variation: For adult parties, substitute 2 bottles (750 ml each) cold sparkling wine for the soda and stir in 1 cup vodka or dark rum and ½ cup triple sec with the apple cider.

Sangria

makes 8 to 10 servings

4 medium oranges, divided
2 lemons, divided
2 bottles (750 ml each) dry red wine
6 ounces triple sec
3 ounces brandy
⅓ to ½ cup sugar
2 cups cold club soda
1 apple, diced

1 Juice 3 oranges and 1 lemon; pour juice into punch bowl. Add wine, liqueur, brandy and sugar to taste; mix well to dissolve sugar. Cover and refrigerate 2 to 6 hours.

2 Just before serving, slice remaining orange and lemon. Stir club soda into sangria; add sliced orange, lemon and apple.

Tropical Fruit Punch

makes about 8 servings

- 2 cups water
- ¾ cup sugar
- 1½ cups cold guava nectar
- 1½ cups cold orange juice
- ½ cup cold pineapple juice
- ¼ cup lime juice
- Ice cubes

1. Combine water and sugar in small saucepan. Cook and stir over medium heat until sugar dissolves. Cool to room temperature.
2. Combine sugar mixture, guava nectar, orange juice, pineapple juice and lime juice in large pitcher; mix well. Serve over ice.

Apple-Berry Punch

makes 8 servings

- 8 to 12 medium fresh strawberries *or* 30 fresh red raspberries
- 7 cups apple juice, divided
- 1 (4-inch) cinnamon stick, broken
- ½ teaspoon whole allspice
- ½ teaspoon vanilla
- 2 cans (12 ounces each) cold lemon-lime soda or ginger ale

1 Cut strawberries in half. Place one strawberry half in each section of three ice cube trays. Spoon about 1 tablespoon of apple juice over each piece of fruit. Freeze until firm.

2 Tie cinnamon and allspice in cheesecloth bag. Combine spice bag and remaining apple juice in large saucepan; bring to a boil. Reduce heat; cover and simmer 5 minutes. Remove from heat; stir in vanilla. Cover and refrigerate 6 hours or until cold.

3 Remove spice bag from apple juice mixture; discard. Pour into large pitcher or small punch bowl. Gently stir in soda and frozen apple juice cubes.

Cardamom Lemonade Spritzer

makes 6 servings

- 3 cups water
- 1¼ cups sugar
- 40 whole white cardamom pods, cracked
- 2 cups lemon juice
- 1 bottle (750 ml) cold Asti Spumante *or* 1 bottle (1 liter) club soda
- Ice cubes

1 Combine water, 1¼ cups sugar and cardamom pods in medium saucepan. Cook and stir over medium heat until sugar dissolves. Reduce heat to low; cover and simmer 30 minutes. Remove from heat; cool completely. Refrigerate 2 hours or up to 3 days.

2 Pour mixture through strainer into large pitcher; discard pods. Stir in lemon juice and Asti Spumante. Serve over ice.

Champagne Punch

makes 6 to 8 servings

- 1 orange
- 1 lemon
- ¼ cup cranberry-flavored liqueur or cognac
- ¼ cup triple sec
- 1 bottle (750 ml) cold sparkling rosé or white wine or champagne
- Fresh cranberries and orange slices

1. Remove colored peel, not white pith, from orange and lemon in long thin strips using citrus peeler. Refrigerate orange and lemon for another use. Combine peels and liqueurs in medium pitcher; refrigerate 2 to 6 hours.
2. Just before serving, tilt pitcher to one side and slowly pour in sparkling wine. (Leave peels in pitcher for added flavor.) Place cranberries in bottom of each champagne glass, if desired. Pour punch into glasses; garnish with orange slices.

Cranberry-Pineapple Punch

makes 8 servings

- 2½ cups cold cranberry juice
- 2 cups cold pineapple juice
- ½ teaspoon almond extract
- 2½ cups cold ginger ale
- Ice cubes
- Fresh cranberries

1. Combine cranberry juice, pineapple juice and almond extract in large pitcher. Gently stir in ginger ale.
2. Serve over ice; garnish with cranberries.

Guava Fruit Punch

makes 4 servings

- 1½ cups boiling water
- 2 decaffeinated black tea bags
- 3 thin slices peeled fresh ginger
- 2 cups cold guava juice
- ¾ cup cold pineapple juice
- 2 tablespoons lemon juice
- Ice cubes

1. Combine boiling water, tea bags and ginger in 2-cup heatproof measuring cup; steep 5 minutes. Discard tea bags and ginger. Cool to room temperature.
2. Add guava juice, pineapple juice and lemon juice to tea mixture; mix well. Serve over ice.

Pomegranate Orange Sangria

makes 10 servings

- 4 medium oranges, divided
- 2 lemons, divided
- 2 bottles (750 ml each) dry red wine
- 8 ounces pomegranate juice
- 6 ounces triple sec
- 3 ounces brandy
- ⅓ cup sugar
- 2 cups cold club soda or seltzer
- 1 apple, sliced
- Pomegranate seeds (arils)

1. Juice 3 oranges and 1 lemon; pour juice into punch bowl. Add wine, pomegranate juice, triple sec, brandy and sugar; stir to dissolve sugar. Cover and refrigerate 2 to 6 hours.
2. Just before serving, slice remaining orange and lemon. Stir club soda into sangria; add orange and lemon slices, apples and pomegranate seeds.

Citrus Punch

makes 8 to 10 servings

- 4 oranges, sectioned
- 1 pint fresh strawberries, stemmed and halved
- 1 to 2 limes, cut into ⅛-inch slices
- 1 lemon, cut into ⅛-inch slices
- 1 cup fresh raspberries
- 2 cups orange juice
- 2 cups grapefruit juice
- ¾ cup lime juice
- ½ cup light corn syrup
- 1 bottle (1 liter) cold ginger ale or white grape juice *or* 1 bottle (750 ml) sparkling wine

1. Spread orange sections, strawberries, lime slices, lemon slices and raspberries on baking sheet. Freeze 4 hours or until firm.
2. Combine juices and corn syrup in large pitcher; stir until corn syrup dissolves. Refrigerate 2 hours or until cold. Stir in ginger ale just before serving.
3. Divide frozen fruit among serving glasses; fill glasses with punch.

Strawberry-Apricot Punch

makes 12 servings

- 2 packages (10 ounces each) frozen sliced strawberries in syrup, thawed
- 2 cans (5½ ounces each) apricot or peach nectar
- ¼ cup lemon juice
- 2 tablespoons honey
- 1 bottle (2 liters) cold lemon-lime soda *or* 2 bottles (750 ml each) sparkling wine

1 Place strawberries with syrup in food processor or blender; process until smooth.

2 Pour puréed strawberries into large punch bowl. Stir in apricot nectar, lemon juice and honey until well blended. Stir in soda just before serving.

Pineapple-Champagne Punch

makes 12 servings

- 1 quart pineapple sherbet
- 1 quart cold pineapple juice
- 1 bottle (750 ml) cold champagne or sparkling wine
- 2 fresh or canned pineapple slices, each cut into 6 wedges

1. Process sherbet and pineapple juice in blender until smooth and frothy. Pour into punch bowl. Stir in champagne.
2. Float pineapple slices in punch; serve immediately.

Coco Loco

makes 1 serving

4 ounces pineapple juice
2 ounces light rum
1 ounce cream of coconut
1 ounce milk
½ ounce amaretto
1 teaspoon grenadine
½ cup ice cubes
Pineapple wedge

Combine pineapple juice, rum, cream of coconut, milk, amaretto, grenadine and ice in blender; blend until smooth. Serve in wine glass; garnish with pineapple wedge.

Blue Hawaii

makes 1 serving

- 3 ounces pineapple juice
- 1 ounce vodka
- 1 ounce light rum
- 1 ounce sour mix, bottled or homemade (recipe follows)
- ½ ounce blue curaçao
- Pineapple wedge

Fill cocktail shaker half full with ice; add pineapple juice, vodka, rum, sour mix and curaçao. Shake until blended; strain into ice-filled hurricane glass. Garnish with pineapple wedge.

Sour Mix: Combine 1 cup water and 1 cup sugar in small saucepan. Cook over medium heat just until sugar is dissolved, stirring frequently. Pour into airtight container; stir in 1 cup lemon juice and ½ cup lime juice. Cool completely; store in refrigerator.

Blue Hawaiian: Omit sour mix and add 1 ounce cream of coconut and 1 teaspoon sugar to cocktail shaker.

Grasshopper

makes 1 serving

2 ounces crème de menthe
2 ounces crème de cacao
2 ounces half-and-half or whipping cream

Fill cocktail shaker half full with ice; add liqueurs and half-and-half. Shake until blended; strain into cocktail glass.

Negroni

makes 1 serving

1 ounce gin
1 ounce Campari
1 ounce sweet vermouth
Orange slice or twist

Fill cocktail shaker half full with ice; add gin, Campari and vermouth. Stir until blended; strain into old fashioned glass. Garnish with orange slice.

Jungle Bird

makes 1 serving

1½ ounces Jamaican or dark aged rum
1½ ounces pineapple juice
¾ ounce Campari
½ ounce lime juice
½ ounce simple syrup (recipe follows)
Pineapple wedge

Fill cocktail shaker half full with ice; add rum, pineapple juice, Campari, lime juice and simple syrup. Shake 30 seconds or until cold; strain into ice-filled old fashioned glass, copper mug or tiki mug. Garnish with pineapple wedge.

Simple Syrup: Combine 1 cup water and 1 cup sugar in small saucepan. Cook over medium heat just until sugar is dissolved, stirring frequently. Cool to room temperature; store syrup in airtight container in refrigerator.

Mimosa

makes 1 serving

4 ounces cold orange juice
4 ounces cold champagne

Pour orange juice into champagne flute; top with champagne.

Boulevardier

makes 1 serving

1½ ounces bourbon
1 ounce sweet vermouth
1 ounce Campari
Orange slice or twist

Fill mixing glass or cocktail shaker half full with ice; add bourbon, vermouth and Campari. Stir 30 seconds or until cold; strain into old fashioned or cocktail glass. Garnish with orange slice.

Classic Margarita

makes 2 servings

Lime wedges
Coarse salt
4 ounces tequila
2 ounces triple sec
2 ounces lime juice
Lime slices or wedges

1 Rub rims of two margarita glasses with lime wedges; dip in salt.

2 Fill cocktail shaker half full with ice; add tequila, triple sec and lime juice. Shake until blended; strain into glasses. Garnish with lime slices.

Frozen Margarita: Rub rim of two margarita glasses with lime wedges; dip in salt. Combine tequila, triple sec, lime juice and 2 cups ice in blender; blend until smooth. Pour into glasses; garnish with lime slices.

Frozen Strawberry Margarita: Rub rim of margarita glasses with lime wedges; dip in salt. Combine tequila, triple sec, lime juice, 1 cup frozen strawberries and 1 cup ice in blender; blend until smooth. Pour into prepared glasses; garnish with lime slices and strawberries.

Eclipse

makes 1 serving

- 2 ounces tequila añejo
- ¾ ounce Aperol
- ¾ ounce cherry liqueur
- ¾ ounce lemon juice
- ¼ ounce mezcal
- Lemon twist

Fill cocktail shaker half full with ice; add tequila, Aperol, liqueur, lemon juice and mezcal. Shake until blended; strain into coupe or old fashioned glass. Garnish with lemon twist.

French 75

makes 1 serving

- 2 ounces gin
- ½ ounce lemon juice
- 1 teaspoon superfine sugar
- 2 ounces chilled champagne or sparkling wine

Fill cocktail shaker half full with ice; add gin, lemon juice and sugar. Shake about 15 seconds or until cold; strain into champagne flute or coupe. Top with champagne; stir gently.

Whiskey Smash

makes 1 serving

2 lemon quarters
8 fresh mint leaves, plus additional for garnish
½ ounce simple syrup (recipe follows)
2 ounces bourbon

Muddle lemon quarters, 8 mint leaves and simple syrup in cocktail shaker. Add bourbon; shake until blended. Strain into old fashioned glass filled with crushed ice; garnish with additional mint.

Simple Syrup: Combine 1 cup water and 1 cup sugar in small saucepan. Cook over medium heat just until sugar is dissolved, stirring frequently. Cool to room temperature; store syrup in airtight container in refrigerator.

Cosmopolitan

makes 1 serving

2 ounces vodka or lemon vodka
1 ounce triple sec
1 ounce cranberry juice
½ ounce lime juice
Orange twist

Fill cocktail shaker half full with ice; add vodka, triple sec and juices. Shake until blended; strain into cocktail glass. Garnish with orange twist.

Cantarito

makes 1 serving

Lime wedge
Coarse salt
1½ ounces tequila
½ ounce lime juice
½ ounce lemon juice
½ ounce orange juice
Grapefruit soda
Lime, lemon and/or orange wedges

Rub rim of Collins glass with lime wedge; dip in salt. Fill glass with ice; add tequila, lime juice, lemon juice and orange juice. Top with soda; stir until blended. Garnish with citrus wedges.

Frozen Mudslide

makes 1 serving

- 1 cup vanilla ice cream
- 1 ounce vodka
- 1 ounce coffee liqueur
- 1 ounce Irish cream liqueur
- 1 to 2 tablespoons whipping cream or half-and-half (optional)
- Chocolate syrup (optional)
- Whipped cream and mini chocolate chips

1. Combine ice cream, vodka, coffee liqueur and Irish cream liqueur in blender; blend until smooth. Add cream, if desired, to reach desired consistency.
2. If desired, garnish glass with chocolate syrup swirls before pouring drink into glass. Hold glass at 90-degree angle; gently squeeze chocolate syrup onto side of glass while turning glass. Or squeeze syrup in vertical squiggles up and down side of glass.
3. Pour drink into prepared glass; garnish with whipped cream and chocolate chips.

Mai Tai

makes 1 serving

1 ounce light rum
1 ounce triple sec
½ ounce grenadine
½ ounce orgeat syrup*
½ ounce lime juice
1 ounce dark rum
Pineapple wedge and maraschino cherry

**Almond-flavored syrup.*

Fill cocktail shaker half full with ice; add light rum, triple sec, grenadine, orgeat syrup and lime juice. Shake until blended; strain into old fashioned glass. Pour dark rum over top (do not stir). Garnish with pineapple wedge and maraschino cherry.

Classic Dry Martini

makes 1 serving

2 ounces gin or vodka
1½ teaspoons dry vermouth
Green olives

Fill cocktail shaker half full with ice; add gin and vermouth. Stir or shake until blended; strain into cocktail glass. Garnish with olives.

Cucumber Punch

makes 10 servings

1 seedless cucumber, thinly sliced
1 cup water
1 can (12 ounces) thawed frozen limeade concentrate
1 bottle (2 liters) cold club soda
Ice cubes
Lime wedges

1. Combine cucumber slices, water and limeade concentrate in punch bowl or pitcher. Refrigerate 1 hour.
2. Add club soda just before serving. Serve over ice; garnish with lime wedges.

Strawberry-Basil Sparklers

makes 8 servings

Basil Simple Syrup (recipe follows)

4 cups fresh strawberries, plus additional for garnish

1 bottle (2 liters) cold club soda

Ice cubes

Fresh basil leaves

1 Prepare Basil Simple Syrup.

2 Combine 4 cups strawberries and Basil Simple Syrup in blender; blend until smooth. Pour into pitcher. Stir in club soda just before serving. Serve over ice; garnish with additional strawberries and basil.

Basil Simple Syrup: Combine 1 cup fresh basil leaves, ⅔ cup sugar and ⅔ cup water in small saucepan; cook and stir over medium heat until sugar is dissolved. Remove from heat; cool completely. Pour through fine-mesh sieve; discard basil. Store in refrigerator up to 1 week.

Snowbird Mocktails

makes 10 servings

3 cups pineapple juice
1 can (14 ounces) sweetened condensed milk
1 can (6 ounces) frozen orange juice concentrate, thawed
½ teaspoon coconut extract
1 bottle (1 liter) cold ginger ale
Orange slices (optional)
Marachino cherries
Crushed ice

1 Combine pineapple juice, sweetened condensed milk, juice concentrate and coconut extract in large pitcher; mix well. Cover and refrigerate at least 1 hour or up to 1 week.

2 Fill 10 glasses with ice. Pour ½ cup pineapple juice mixture into each glass; top each with ⅓ cup ginger ale. Garnish with orange slices and cherries.

Kiwi Lemonade

makes 5 servings

¾ cup sugar
3 cups water, divided
1 cup lemon juice
2 kiwis

1. Combine sugar and ½ cup water in small saucepan; cook over medium heat until sugar is dissolved. Remove from heat; cool slightly.
2. Combine lemon juice, remaining 2½ cups water and sugar syrup in pitcher. Refrigerate until cold.
3. Peel kiwis and coarsely chop. Add to blender or food processor; blend until smooth. Strain into lemonade; stir until well blended. Refrigerate until cold. Serve over ice.

Strawberry Lemonade

makes 5 servings

- 3 cups water, divided
- 1 cup sugar
- 1 cup frozen strawberries
- 1½ cups lemon juice

1. Combine 1 cup water, sugar and strawberries in small saucepan; bring to a boil over high heat. Boil 5 minutes. Remove from heat; cool completely.
2. Pour strawberry mixture into blender; blend until smooth. Strain into pitcher. Stir in lemon juice and remaining 2 cups water until blended. Refrigerate until cold.

Sparkling Pomegranate Gingerade

makes 4 servings

- ½ cup sugar
- ¼ cup water
- 1 teaspoon grated lemon peel
- 1 (1-inch) piece fresh ginger, thinly sliced
- 2 cups cold seltzer water
- 2 cups cold pomegranate juice
- Ice cubes

1. Combine sugar, water, lemon peel and ginger in small saucepan; bring to a boil over medium heat. Boil 1 minute. Remove from heat; cool completely.
2. Strain syrup into large pitcher; discard solids. Stir in seltzer and pomegranate juice just before serving. Serve over ice.

Frozen Lemonade Iced Tea

makes 2 servings

- ¼ cup sweetened powdered iced tea mix
- 1¼ cups cold water, divided
- 1½ cups ice cubes
- 1 cup lemon sorbet
- ¼ cup frozen lemonade concentrate

1 Combine tea mix and ¼ cup cold water in blender. Add ice; blend until slushy. Pour into two tall glasses.

2 Add sorbet, remaining 1 cup water and lemonade concentrate to blender; blend until smooth. Pour over tea mixture in glasses.

Pomegranate Lemon Refresher

makes 4 servings

- 3 bags hibiscus-lemon tea
- 1½ cups boiling water
- ⅓ cup sugar
- 3 tablespoons lemon juice
- 1½ cups pomegranate juice
- 1 cup cold club soda
- Ice cubes
- Lemon wedges

1 Place tea bags in teapot or 2-cup heatproof measuring cup. Add boiling water; steep tea 5 minutes. Remove and discard tea bags. Stir in sugar until dissolved; cool to room temperature. Refrigerate until cold.

2 Combine tea, lemon juice and pomegranate juice in pitcher; mix well.

3 Just before serving, stir in club soda. Serve over ice; garnish with lemon wedges.

Raspberry Lemonade Slushies

makes 6 servings

- 1½ cups fresh or frozen raspberries
- 1 can (6 ounces) frozen lemonade concentrate
- 1 cup water
- 4 cups ice cubes
- Lemon wedges

1. Combine raspberries, lemonade concentrate and water in blender or food processor; blend until smooth. Add ice; blend until smooth.
2. Pour into six glasses. Garnish with lemon wedges; serve immediately.

Almond Choco-tini

makes 4 servings

8 ounces cream of coconut
8 ounces milk
5 ounces chocolate syrup
1 teaspoon almond extract
3 cups ice cubes
Chocolate shavings

1 Combine cream of coconut, milk, chocolate syrup, almond extract and ice in blender; blend until smooth.

2 Pour into cocktail glasses; garnish with chocolate shavings.

Chilled Lemon Sunset

makes 4 servings

1½ cups water, divided
½ cup sugar
1 pint (2 cups) lemon sorbet
½ cup orange juice
¼ cup lemon juice
4 teaspoons grenadine
4 lemon slices

1 Combine ½ cup water and sugar in small saucepan. Cook and stir over medium heat until sugar dissolves. Pour mixture into 2-cup heatproof measuring cup. Cool to room temperature; refrigerate 1 hour.

2 Combine remaining 1 cup water, sugar syrup, sorbet, orange juice, and lemon juice in blender; blend until smooth.

3 Pour 1 teaspoon grenadine into bottom of each of four glasses; top with sorbet mixture. Garnish with lemon slices; serve immediately.

Ginger Apple Spritzer

makes 4 to 6 servings

- 3 English breakfast tea bags
- 1 cup boiling water
- ¼ cup sugar
- 2 tablespoons minced crystallized ginger
- 2 tablespoons lemon juice
- 3 cups cold sparkling apple cider
- Ice cubes
- Lemon wedges

1 Place tea bags in 2-cup heatproof measuring cup. Add boiling water; steep 5 minutes. Remove and discard tea bags. Stir in sugar until dissolved. Cool to room temperature; refrigerate until cold.

2 Combine tea, ginger and lemon juice in pitcher; mix well.

3 Just before serving, stir in sparkling cider. Serve over ice; garnish with lemon wedges.

Crushed Kiddie Cocktail

makes 4 servings

1 jar (6 ounces) maraschino cherries
2 cups lemon sorbet
¼ cup frozen lemonade concentrate
½ cup cold lemon-lime soda
½ cup crushed ice

1 Reserve 4 cherries. Pour remaining cherries and half of juice from jar into blender; blend until smooth. Divide among four glasses.

2 Rinse out blender. Combine sorbet, lemonade concentrate, soda and ice in blender; blend until smooth. Pour over cherry mixture in glasses. Garnish with reserved cherries.

Cuban Batido

makes 2 servings

- 1½ cups cubed fresh pineapple
- ¾ cup milk
- ½ cup orange juice
- 3 tablespoons sugar
- 1 tablespoon lime juice
- 1 cup ice cubes
- Lime slices

1. Combine pineapple, milk, orange juice, sugar, lime juice and ice in blender; blend until smooth.
2. Pour into two glasses. Garnish with lime slices; serve immediately.

Turtle Tornado

makes 4 servings

1½ cups chocolate frozen yogurt or ice cream

¾ cup vanilla frozen yogurt or ice cream

¾ cup milk

¼ cup caramel ice cream topping, plus additional for garnish

¼ cup chocolate chips, plus additional for garnish

1 Combine frozen yogurts, milk, ¼ cup caramel topping and ¼ cup chocolate chips in blender; blend until smooth.

2 Pour into four glasses. Sprinkle each with additional chocolate chips and drizzle with additional caramel topping.

Cookies and Cream Shake

makes 1 serving

- **5 chocolate sandwich cookies, divided**
- **¼ cup milk**
- **2 cups vanilla ice cream**
- **Whipped cream or whipped topping**

1. Coarsely chop four cookies. Chop remaining cookie into smaller pieces; set aside for garnish.
2. Pour milk into blender; add ice cream and blend just until smooth. Add coarsely chopped cookies; pulse until blended.
3. Pour into glass. Top with whipped cream and reserved cookie pieces; serve immediately.

Orange Whip

makes 2 servings

- 2 cups ice cubes
- 1 can (12 ounces) frozen orange juice concentrate with pulp, partially thawed
- 1 cup milk
- ¼ cup powdered sugar
- ½ teaspoon vanilla

1. Combine ice, juice concentrate, milk, powdered sugar and vanilla in blender; pulse to break up ice. Blend until smooth.
2. Pour into two glasses; serve immediately.

Chocolate Cake Shake

makes 1 serving

- **1 slice (⅛ of cake) Chocolate Cake (recipe follows)**
- **½ cup milk**
- **1 cup vanilla ice cream**

1. Prepare Chocolate Cake.
2. Combine milk, ice cream and cake slice in blender; blend just until cake is incorporated but texture of shake is not completely smooth. Pour into glass; serve immediately.

Chocolate Cake

makes 8 servings

- **1 package (about 15 ounces) devil's food cake mix**
- **1 cup cold water**
- **1 cup mayonnaise**
- **3 eggs**
- **1½ containers (16 ounces each) chocolate frosting**

1. Preheat oven to 350°F. Grease two 9-inch round cake pans.
2. Beat cake mix, water, mayonnaise and eggs in large bowl with electric mixer at low speed 30 seconds. Beat at medium speed 2 minutes. Pour batter into prepared pans.
3. Bake 25 minutes or until toothpick inserted into centers comes out clean. Cool in pans 10 minutes. Remove to wire rack; cool completely.
4. Fill and frost cake with chocolate frosting.

Frosted Lemonade

makes 3 servings

½ cup sugar
3 cups water, divided
1 cup lemon juice
6 cups vanilla ice cream
Lemon slices

1 Combine sugar and ½ cup water in small saucepan. Cook and stir over medium heat until sugar dissolves.

2 Combine lemon juice, remaining 2½ cups water and sugar syrup in pitcher or large measuring cup. Refrigerate until cold.

3 For each serving, combine 1 cup lemonade and 2 cups ice cream in blender; blend until smooth. Pour into glasses. Garnish with lemon wedge; serve immediately.

Minty Green Shake

makes 1 serving

2 cups French vanilla ice cream
½ cup milk, divided
⅛ teaspoon peppermint extract
10 drops green food coloring
Whipped cream and maraschino cherry

1 Combine ice cream, ¼ cup milk, peppermint extract and green food coloring in blender; blend until smooth. Add additional ¼ cup milk if needed to reach desired consistency.

2 Pour into glass. Garnish with whipped cream and cherry; serve immediately.

Banana Nut Bread in a Glass

makes 4 servings

- 1 cup pecan or walnut pieces
- 2 cups milk
- 5 bananas
- 3 tablespoons sugar
- 3 tablespoons brown sugar corn syrup
- ¼ teaspoon ground nutmeg
- Whipped cream

1. Cook pecans in small skillet over medium heat 5 minutes or until lightly toasted and fragrant, stirring occasionally. Spread on plate; cool 5 minutes.
2. Place nuts, milk, bananas, sugar, corn syrup and nutmeg in blender; blend until smooth.
3. Pour into four glasses. Top with whipped cream; serve immediately.

Root Beer Float Shake

makes 1 serving

1 cup vanilla ice cream or frozen yogurt

1 cup root beer

½ teaspoon vanilla

Whipped cream and crushed root beer-flavored hard candy

1. Place glass mug in freezer at least 1 hour before serving, if desired.
2. Combine ice cream, root beer and vanilla in blender; blend until smooth. Pour in frozen mug or glass. Top with whipped cream and candy, if desired; serve immediately.

Note: For extra root beer flavor, add up to 1 teaspoon root beer extract to the shake with the vanilla. Most grocery stores sell root beer extract in the baking aisle by the spices, extracts and flavorings.

Double Strawberry Shake

makes 4 servings

- **2 cups strawberry ice cream**
- **1 cup sliced fresh strawberries, plus additional for garnish**
- **⅔ cup cold milk**
- **¼ cup cold orange juice**
- **⅛ teaspoon ground cinnamon**

1 Place ice cream, 1 cup strawberries, milk, orange juice and cinnamon in blender. Blend until smooth.

2 Pour into glasses. Garnish with additional strawberries; serve immediately.

Key Lime Chiller

makes 4 servings

- 2 cups vanilla ice cream
- ⅔ cup frozen limeade concentrate
- 1 graham cracker, broken into pieces, plus additional for garnish
- ¼ cup milk
- Lime slices

1. Combine ice cream, limeade concentrate and milk in blender; blend until smooth. Add 1 graham cracker; pulse until just combined.
2. Pour into four glasses. Garnish with lime slices and additional cracker pieces; serve immediately.

Chipotle Chili-Spiked Mocha Slush

makes 2 servings

- **1 package (1 to 1¼ ounces) instant hot chocolate mix without marshmallows**
- **½ teaspoon instant coffee granules**
- **⅛ teaspoon chipotle chili powder**
- **⅛ teaspoon ground cinnamon**
- **¾ cup hot water**
- **1 cup coffee, vanilla or chocolate ice cream**
- **⅓ cup half-and-half**
- **Whipped cream**

1 Combine hot chocolate mix, coffee granules, chipotle chili powder and cinnamon in 2-cup glass measure. Stir in hot water until blended. Pour into ice cube tray. Freeze until firm.

2 Combine chocolate ice cubes, ice cream and half-and-half in blender; blend until smooth.

3 Pour into two glasses. Garnish with whipped cream; serve immediately.

Peanut Butter and Jelly Shakes

makes 2 servings

1½ cups vanilla ice cream
¼ cup milk
2 tablespoons creamy peanut butter
6 peanut butter sandwich cookies, coarsely chopped
¼ cup strawberry preserves
1 to 2 teaspoons water

1 Combine ice cream, milk and peanut butter in blender; blend until smooth. Add chopped cookies; process 10 seconds.

2 Pour into two glasses. Place preserves and water in small bowl; stir until smooth. Stir 2 tablespoons preserve mixture into each glass. Serve immediately.

Sky Blue Fluffer Slusher

makes 4 servings

1 package (4-serving size) berry blue gelatin mix
1 cup very cold water
2 cups crushed ice
1 jar (7 ounces) marshmallow creme
¼ cup mini marshmallows
4 maraschino cherries

1 Dissolve gelatin in cold water in medium bowl.

2 Combine gelatin mixture, crushed ice and marshmallow creme in blender; blend until mixture is slushy.

3 Pour into four glasses. Sprinkle each serving with mini marshmallows and top with a cherry, if desired; serve immediately.

Espresso Shake

makes 3 servings

1½ cups vanilla ice cream
1 cup whipping cream
1 tablespoon instant espresso powder
½ teaspoon vanilla

1 Combine ice cream, whipping cream, espresso powder and vanilla in blender. Process until smooth.

2 Pour into three glasses; serve immediately.

Lemon Chiffon Cooler

makes 4 servings

- 2 cups milk
- 2 cups (1 pint) lemon sorbet, softened
- 1 cup French vanilla ice cream
- 2 teaspoons grated lemon peel, plus additional for garnish
- ⅓ cup lemon juice
- 1 tablespoon sugar
- Whipped cream

1 Combine milk, sorbet, ice cream, 2 teaspoons lemon peel, lemon juice and sugar in blender. Process until smooth.

2 Pour into four glasses. Top with whipped cream and sprinkle of lemon peel; serve immediately.

Tip: When grating lemon peel, be sure to use only the yellow part of the peel and not the bitter white part. Grate the peel before you juice the lemon.

Tiramisu Shake

makes 4 servings

- 1½ cups chocolate ice cream or frozen yogurt
- ½ cup cold brewed espresso or strong coffee
- 8 ounces mascarpone cheese
- ¾ cup vanilla ice cream or frozen yogurt
- ¼ cup half-and-half
- 1 tablespoon powdered sugar
- 1 tablespoon unsweetened cocoa powder
- Pirouette cookies or thin biscotti

1. Combine chocolate ice cream and espresso in blender; blend until smooth. Pour into four glasses.
2. Rinse out blender. Combine mascarpone, vanilla ice cream and half-and-half in blender; blend until smooth. Pour over chocolate mixture.
3. Mix powdered sugar and cocoa in small bowl. Sift mixture over each glass. Garnish with pirouette cookies; serve immediately.

Chocolate Chip Cookie Shake

makes 4 servings

- 3 cups French vanilla ice cream
- 2 cups milk
- ½ cup packed brown sugar
- 1 teaspoon vanilla
- 2 ounces semisweet chocolate, grated
- Chocolate curls

1. Combine ice cream, milk, brown sugar and vanilla in blender; blend until smooth.
2. Add chocolate; process just until combined. Pour into four glasses. Garnish with chocolate curls; serve immediately.

Strawberry Sundae Shake

makes 4 servings

10 ounces frozen unsweetened strawberries, thawed
2 cups vanilla ice cream
1 cup milk
2 bananas
2 tablespoons sugar
1 cup ice cubes
Whipped cream, chocolate syrup and candy sprinkles

1 Combine strawberries, ice cream, milk, bananas, sugar and ice in blender; blend until smooth.

2 Pour into four glasses. Top with whipped cream, chocolate syrup and sprinkles, if desired; serve immediately.

HOT DRINKS

Hot Toddies

makes 10 servings

8 cups water
¾ cup honey
⅔ cup lemon juice
1 (1-inch) piece ginger, peeled and cut into 4 slices
1 cinnamon stick
2 cups bourbon
Lemon slices

1 Combine water, honey, lemon juice, ginger and cinnamon stick in medium saucepan. Bring to a boil over medium-high heat. Reduce heat to low; cover and simmer 30 minutes. Remove from heat; stir in bourbon.

2 Remove and discard cinnamon stick and ginger pieces. Ladle into individual mugs; garnish with lemon slices.

Triple Delicious Hot Chocolate

makes 6 servings

3 cups milk, divided
⅓ cup sugar
¼ cup unsweetened cocoa powder
¼ teaspoon salt
¾ teaspoon vanilla
1 cup whipping cream
1 ounce white chocolate, chopped
1 ounce bittersweet chocolate, chopped
Whipped cream
3 teaspoons mini chocolate chips or shaved bittersweet chocolate

1 Combine ½ cup milk, sugar, cocoa and salt in medium saucepan; whisk until smooth. Whisk in remaining 2½ cups milk and vanilla. Cook over medium heat until hot but not boiling.

2 Stir in cream, white chocolate and bittersweet chocolate until melted and smooth.

3 Pour hot chocolate into mugs. Top with whipped cream and chocolate chips.

Mulled Apple Cider

makes 10 servings

- 8 whole allspice berries
- 4 cinnamon sticks, broken into halves, plus additional for garnish
- 1 square (8 inches) double-thickness cheesecloth
- 12 whole cloves
- 1 large orange
- 2 quarts (8 cups) apple cider
- ¼ cup packed brown sugar

1. Wrap allspice berries and cinnamon stick halves in cheesecloth; tie securely with cotton string or strip of cheesecloth. Stick cloves randomly into orange; cut orange into quarters.
2. Combine apple cider and brown sugar in medium saucepan; add spice bag and orange quarters. Cover and cook over medium heat 1 hour.
3. Remove and discard spice bag and orange. Ladle cider into mugs; garnish with additional cinnamon sticks.

Mulled Wine

makes 6 to 8 servings

- 2 bottles (750 ml each) dry red wine
- 1 orange, sliced
- ¼ cup brandy
- ¼ cup sugar
- 10 whole cloves
- 2 cinnamon sticks
- 2 star anise
- Lemon slices

1 Combine wine, orange, brandy, sugar, cloves, cinnamon sticks and star anise in large saucepan; bring to a simmer over medium-low heat. (Do not boil or allow temperature to exceed 170°F.) Simmer 1 hour. Strain before serving.

2 Pour into mugs; garnish with lemon slices.

Brandied Cranapple Punch

makes 6 to 8 servings

- 1½ quarts (6 cups) cranapple juice cocktail
- 2 oranges, thinly sliced, divided
- ¼ cup packed brown sugar
- 3 cinnamon sticks
- 12 whole cloves
- 2 star anise
- 1 cup brandy or cognac

1. Combine juice, 1 orange, brown sugar, cinnamon, cloves and star anise in large saucepan. Bring to a simmer over medium heat. Reduce heat to low; cover and simmer 30 minutes. Remove from heat; add brandy.
2. Ladle into mugs, leaving spices in saucepan. Garnish with remaining orange slices.

Zesty Hot Cocoa Mix

makes about 2½ cups mix (10 servings)

- 6 ounces dark chocolate, chopped *or* 1 cup bittersweet chocolate chips
- 1 cup nonfat dry milk
- ¼ cup sugar
- 2 tablespoons unsweetened cocoa powder
- 1 tablespoon cornstarch
- 2 teaspoons ground cinnamon
- ¼ to ½ teaspoon mild red chili powder
- ⅛ teaspoon ground cloves
- Water or milk

1. Place chocolate pieces in food processor; pulse until chocolate resembles coarse powder. Place in medium bowl. Add milk, sugar, cocoa, cornstarch, cinnamon, chili powder and cloves; whisk until well blended. Store in airtight container.
2. For each serving, combine ¼ cup cocoa mix and 1 cup water or milk in small saucepan. Heat over medium-low heat until slightly thickened and hot but not boiling, stirring occasionally. Pour into mug.

Hot Spiced Cider

makes 1 quart cider and 6 spice bags

Mulling Spice Bags

- 1 package cheesecloth
- 12 cinnamon sticks, broken into 1-inch pieces
- ¼ cup allspice berries (about ¾ ounce)
- ¼ cup whole cloves (about ¾ ounce)
- 1 tablespoon grated dried lemon peel
- 1 tablespoon grated dried orange peel
- 1 tablespoon ground cardamom
- 1 tablespoon ground nutmeg
- 6 (12-inch) lengths food-safe twine or string

Cider

- 1 quart apple cider

1 Cut six 6-inch squares of cheesecloth. Combine cinnamon sticks, allspice, cloves, lemon peel, orange peel, cardamom and nutmeg in medium bowl. Divide mixture equally among cheesecloth squares, about ¼ cup per square. Bring corners of squares together and tuck in any loose edges. Tie each bag tightly with twine.

2 Heat apple cider and one mulling spice bag in medium saucepan over medium heat about 10 minutes or until cider is hot but not boiling. Serve in mugs. Store remaining spice bags in airtight container.

Minty Rich Cocoa Mix

makes 4 cups mix (16 servings)

- 1½ cups powdered nondairy creamer
- 1 cup nonfat dry milk
- ½ cup granulated sugar
- 6 tablespoons unsweetened cocoa powder
- ¼ cup packed brown sugar
- ¼ teaspoon salt
- 16 peppermint sticks, coarsely crushed*
- 1 cup milk chocolate chips
- Boiling water
- Whipped cream

**Place in heavy-duty resealable food storage bag. Gently pound with rolling pin or flat side of meat mallet until coarsely crushed.*

1. Combine creamer, milk, granulated sugar, cocoa, brown sugar and salt in medium bowl; whisk until well blended. Stir in peppermint and chocolate chips.
2. For each serving, place ¼ cup cocoa mix in mug. Add ¾ cup boiling water; stir until chocolate is melted and peppermint is dissolved. Garnish with whipped cream. Store remaining mix in airtight container.

INDEX

INDEX

INDEX

INDEX

Metric Conversion Chart

VOLUME MEASUREMENTS (dry)

1/8 teaspoon = 0.5 mL
1/4 teaspoon = 1 mL
1/2 teaspoon = 2 mL
3/4 teaspoon = 4 mL
1 teaspoon = 5 mL
1 tablespoon = 15 mL
2 tablespoons = 30 mL
1/4 cup = 60 mL
1/3 cup = 75 mL
1/2 cup = 125 mL
2/3 cup = 150 mL
3/4 cup = 175 mL
1 cup = 250 mL
2 cups = 1 pint = 500 mL
3 cups = 750 mL
4 cups = 1 quart = 1 L

VOLUME MEASUREMENTS (fluid)

1 fluid ounce (2 tablespoons) = 30 mL
4 fluid ounces (1/2 cup) = 125 mL
8 fluid ounces (1 cup) = 250 mL
12 fluid ounces (1 1/2 cups) = 375 mL
16 fluid ounces (2 cups) = 500 mL

WEIGHTS (mass)

1/2 ounce = 15 g
1 ounce = 30 g
3 ounces = 90 g
4 ounces = 120 g
8 ounces = 225 g
10 ounces = 285 g
12 ounces = 360 g
16 ounces = 1 pound = 450 g

DIMENSIONS

1/16 inch = 2 mm
1/8 inch = 3 mm
1/4 inch = 6 mm
1/2 inch = 1.5 cm
3/4 inch = 2 cm
1 inch = 2.5 cm

OVEN TEMPERATURES

250°F = 120°C
275°F = 140°C
300°F = 150°C
325°F = 160°C
350°F = 180°C
375°F = 190°C
400°F = 200°C
425°F = 220°C
450°F = 230°C

BAKING PAN SIZES

Utensil	Size in Inches/Quarts	Metric Volume	Size in Centimeters
Baking or Cake Pan (square or rectangular)	8×8×2	2 L	20×20×5
	9×9×2	2.5 L	23×23×5
	12×8×2	3 L	30×20×5
	13×9×2	3.5 L	33×23×5
Loaf Pan	8×4×3	1.5 L	20×10×7
	9×5×3	2 L	23×13×7
Round Layer Cake Pan	8×1½	1.2 L	20×4
	9×1½	1.5 L	23×4
Pie Plate	8×1¼	750 mL	20×3
	9×1¼	1 L	23×3
Baking Dish or Casserole	1 quart	1 L	—
	1½ quart	1.5 L	—
	2 quart	2 L	—